Anonymous

Representation and petition from His Highness The Nabob of the Carnatic : presented to the House of Commons, March 5, 1792

Anonymous

Representation and petition from His Highness The Nabob of the Carnatic : presented to the House of Commons, March 5, 1792

ISBN/EAN: 9783337156787

Printed in Europe, USA, Canada, Australia, Japan

Cover: Foto ©ninafisch / pixelio.de

REPRESENTATION

AND

PETITION

FROM HIS HIGHNESS

The Nabob of the Carnatic,

PRESENTED TO THE

HOUSE OF COMMONS

MARCH 5, 1792.

LONDON:

PRINTED FOR J. DEBRETT, OPPOSITE BURLINGTON-HOUSE, PICCADILLY.

M,DCC.XCII.

INTRODUCTION.

IN order the better to comprehend the principal ſubject of complaint in the following Petition, it may not be unacceptable to ſtate very ſhortly the circumſtances that have occurred in India, in the laſt and in the preſent War.

In the laſt War, the Nabob aſſigned over his Country to Lord *Macartney* upon certain conditions, for three or five years; and Mr. *Haſtings* earneſtly recommended it to his Lordſhip to appropriate *all the reſources of Tanjore* to the Public Service during the War, except ſuch parts of thoſe reſources as ſhould be required for the Rajah's ſubſiſtence.

The ceſſion of the Carnatic being a *voluntary act* on the part of the Nabob, does not seem to have attracted the attention of Parliament; but the *sentiments* expressed by Mr. *Hastings* relative to Tanjore, very *strongly* excited the notice of Mr. *Dundas*, who moved the following Resolution, which the House, in the *Rockingham* Administration, *unanimously voted*.

29th *April*, 1782. "That any attempt to seize upon the revenues of "the kingdom of Tanjore, and to confiscate the same for the purpose of "the Nabob, or of the East-India Company, *is contrary to the Public faith*, "and tends to the *oppression* and *ruin* of "the Company."

28th *May*, 1782. "That if any "person, *in violation of the Public faith*, "given by the East-India Company in "1775, and contrary to the *true intent* "*and meaning* of the several Resolu-

"tions

" tions of this Houſe, of the 29th of " April laſt. have taken in ſequeſtration, " or *otherwiſe*, the revenues of Tanjore " into the management of the *Nabob* " *of Arcot, or of the Eaſt-India Company*, " it is the *duty* of the Court of Direc- " tors *forthwith*, to order the ſaid reve- " nues to be *returned to the Adminiſtra-* " *tion of the King of Tanjore, agreeable* " *to the Treaties of* 1762 and 1775."

We have inſerted theſe Reſolutions to ſhew of how much *importance* it appeared to be in the opinion of Mr. *Dundas*, and of the Houſe of Commons, that *Treaties* ſhould be inviolably adhered to.

In the year 1784, the Board of Controul directed the Government of Fort St. George, to *reſtore to the* management of the Nabob, the revenues of the Carnatic, and they acknowledged him to be the Sovereign of the Country. It appears, that between the month of December, 1781, when the Nabob aſſigned the Carnatic to Lord *Macartney* during the War, and the month of September, 1784, when the Board of Controul ordered his country to be reſtored to him, the Nabob had repeatedly complained that the conditions on which he had aſſigned his country had not been preſerved. Whether this complaint was well or ill founded is now of no conſequence, as, from the month of February, 1787, the Nabob and the Company entered into a *new Treaty*, and it is of the violation of *that Treaty*, his Highneſs now complains.

After a long and intricate negociation, Sir *Archibald Campbell*, on the 24th of February, 1787, ſigned *a Treaty of perpetual friendſhip, alliance* and *ſecurity* with the Nabob, in the preſence of Sir

John

John Macpherſon and Mr. *Stables*, who were then at Fort St. George, in their way to England.

This Treaty was concluded under the orders of the Board of Controul. It is drawn up with remarkable perſpecuity, and the object and ſcope of the Treaty is ſo evident, that no man can miſtake it.

Sir Archibald Campbell laboured to ſecure for the Company, in time of peace, the payment of a fixed ſum annually, for the ſupport of the military eſtabliſhment on the coaſt; and in war, to ſecure the payment of four-fifths of all the revenues produced in the Carnatic.

The Nabob, *on his part*, laboured ſo to ſecure his own honour and dignity, that without a *direct* and *flagrant* violation of *public faith*, no *poſſible contingency could* ariſe, that ſhould deprive him of the

the *ſovereignty* and management of the Carnatic, either in peace or war.

The Treaty therefore contains the following *poſitive* conditions.

I. That the Nabob ſhall pay a ſpecific ſum annually, for the ſupport of the military peace eſtabliſhment.

II. That in time of war, he ſhall appropriate four-fifths of his revenues to ſupport the war.

But ſhould the Nabob fall in *arrear* in his payments *in peace*, certain ſpecified diſtricts are to be delivered over to the Company, until the arrear ſhall be paid up; the Company are to receive the revenues of thoſe diſtricts, *from the Nabob's Aumils*; if the Aumils behave ill, the Nabob ſhall diſmiſs them, and appoint ſuch others as the Company approve of.

In

In war the Company are allowed to ſend inſpectors, to ſee that four-fifths of his revenues are *honeſtly* appropriated. He has the ſame *privilege* in war, relative to the countries *in our poſſeſſion.* The Company have alſo the privilege, in war, to ſend *ſuperintendants*, to receive the revenues from the *Nabob's Aumils.*

The Treaty then ſtates " That the " exerciſe of power over the ſaid diſ- " tricts, in caſe of failure, ſhall not " *extend*, or be conſtrued to *extend*, " to *deprive* his Highneſs the Na- " bob of the Carnatic, in behalf of " himſelf or his ſucceſſors, of the *civil* " *government thereof*, the credit of his " family, or the dignity *of his illuſtrious* " *houſe*; but that the ſame ſhall be pre- " ſerved to *him*, and *them inviolable*, " *ſaving* and *excepting* the *powers* in the " foregoing

" foregoing article *expreſſed* and *men-*
" *tioned.*"

It is alſo ſtipulated in the Treaty, that the Company ſhall communicate all their negociations, in which the intereſt of the Carnatic ſhall be concerned, to the Nabob; and that his name ſhall be inſerted in all Treaties, relative to the Carnatic.

It is alſo agreed, that if the revenue of the Carnatic, in time of peace, ſhould fall ſhort, in conſequence of a want of rain, or any other unforeſeen calamity, a proportional reduction ſhall be made from the amount of the ſum he had ſtipulated to pay.

This Treaty received the fulleſt *approbation* of the Board of Controul, under whoſe *orders* it was in fact concluded.

Sir

Sir *Archibald Campbell*, when he ſent home the Treaty, ſpeaks in the following terms of the Nabob.

" I have *narrowly watched* all the " Nabob's *conduct* and *ſentiments* ſince " my arrival in this country, and I am " ready to *declare* that I do not think it " *poſſible* that any *Prince*, or Power *on* " *earth*, can be more ſincerely attached " to the proſperity of the Honourable " Company than his Highneſs, *or that* " *any one has a higher claim to their fa-* " *vour and liberality.*

Sir *Archibald Campbell* was ſucceeded in his government by Mr. *Hollond* in 1789, and in the month of March 1790, General *Medows* arrived. The war with *Tippoo* was then *determined upon*, though not *commenced* until *June*.

The General, on the 31st of March 1790, writes in the following terms to the court of Directors:

"We have a long arrear both from "and to us. His Highness the Nabob "is so backward in his payments, and "oppressive to his Poligars, that at this "time it is so necessary to have on "our side, that *I conceive* it will "be *absolutely necessary* upon his first "material delay of payment, *to take* "*the management of his country into* "*your own hands*; a measure, in spite "of the opposition to it, so advantageous "to you, to the country, and even to his "Highness himself, when so wisely pro-"jected and ably executed by Lord "Macartney."

The arrear due at this time was six and a half lacks of pagodas. The Nabob on his part required a deduction for bad

bad ſeaſons, *agreeably to the* letter of the treaty; but admitting the Nabob to owe *any ſum whatever*, the Treaty had provided a remedy. The conſtruction therefore to be put upon the General's letter is this, that for *political purpoſes*, he conceived it abſolutely neceſſary to ſeize the government of the Carnatic, in violation of the Treaty.

In the ſubſequent ſtages of this buſineſs, the *principles* upon which the Government of Fort St. George acted, are very fully explained.

In the letter from the Madras Government to the Court of Directors, which is before the Houſe of Commons, they detailed the various applications that they had made to the Nabob, for the balance due to them, according to the ſtipulations in Sir A. Campbell's Treaty; and war being in fact inevitable, and their army equipping for the field, they *candidly* and *fairly* ſay (in their letter to Bengal), " We proceeded to remark *on* " *the inſufficiency* of the ſtipulations *in* " *Sir Archbibald Campbell's treaty*, to ſe- " cure the regular receipt of 4-5ths of " the Nabob's revenues, agreed to be " paid to the Company's treaſury, *in the* " *event of war*."

They ſay further, " With this view " we pointed out to his Lordſhip in " council, *the impolicy of depending for* " *our principal reſources*, at a time *when* " *the greateſt exertions were neceſſary, and* " *pecuniary ſupplies of the utmoſt import-* " *ance*, upon *the operation and manage-* " *ment of the* Nabob's Government, of " which the ſyſtem was perhaps as de- " fective and inſufficient as any upon " earth; and we did not heſitate to de- " clare it, *as our unqualified opinion*, that " this

" this Government *ought*, during the
" war, *to take the Nabob's country under*
" *their own management*, as affording
" the only means by which the reſources
" to be derived from it could be realiz-
" ed, and the fidelity and attachment
" of the Polegars, and tributaries ſe-
" cured, which is of the utmoſt impor-
" tance to the ſucceſsful operations of
" the war.

" In the event of his Lordſhip's
" agreeing with us in opinion, and in-
" ſtructing us to act in conformity, we
" ſubmitted to him the *neceſſity* of our
" adopting the meaſure, *in ſo comprehen-*
" *ſive a manner, as to preclude any kind*
" *of interference on the part of the Nabob,*
" *while* the country was under our ma-
" nagement; and ſtating, that if this
" *were not done, the expected advantages*
" *would not be derived.*"

12th May,

12th May, 1790, " It might have " been *expected*, that the ſecurities for " the performance of the war ſtipula- " tions, which are of ſuch importance, " would have been made *ſtronger* than " thoſe which are provided in the event " of failures in the time of peace; but " they are, in fact, *leſs efficient*, and the " proceſs preſcribed for failures in time " of war, is ſo tedious and complicated, " *that it can ſcarce be ſaid to deſerve the* " *name of any ſecurity or proviſion what-* " *ever.*"

The Madras Government firſt endeavoured to *perſuade* the Nabob to reſign his Government during the war, and until the arrears were paid off. This, as it was very natural to believe, was a vain attempt. He profeſſed the utmoſt aſtoniſhment at the attempt, but offered to receive inſpectors, agreeably to the

letter

letter and ſpirit of Sir *Archibald Campbell's* Treaty. We have entered *the reaſons* aſſigned by the Madras Government for preſſing Earl *Cornwallis* to aſſent to their ſeizure of the Carnatic—the arguments, however *ſtrong*, are ſuch as a Houſe of Commons cannot *endure* upon the *principles* on which they voted the Reſolutions of April and May, 1782, or upon the principles on which they voted to impeach Mr. *Haſtings* for an alledged breach of faith, not ſaid to be committed by him, when it was in his option to have war or not, but when war actually raged in every part of India, and when the Public expences were moſt preſſing.

After various repreſentations to Bengal, the country was at laſt ſeized, in ſpite of the ſtrongeſt remonſtrances of the Nabob. Of the ſeizure, the following

lowing Petition complains, but the ſubject has often been agitated in the Houſe of Commons.

The friends of Mr. *Haſtings*, have uſed it as an *argumentum ad hominem againſt* Mr. *Dundas*, without going into the ſubject with any other view. Mr. *Dundas* has, on his part, *denied that* there had been any breach of Treaty; and very freely did confeſs that he ſhould be barred from every plea of defence if he could conſent to impeach Mr. *Haſtings*, for a violation of faith, and approve of the ſame conduct in others. In this aſſertion he manifeſtly differs from the Government of Madras, who do not conceal that they have broken the Treaty, but aſſign as a reaſon, that the Treaty itſelf was *inefficient*.

All the papers on this ſubject are now ordered to be printed, and if theſe remarks

marks ſhould be honoured with any attention by Members of Parliament, all the Writer hopes or wiſhes is this, that it may induce them to read thoſe Papers, and then he is *confident* there cannot be *two opinions upon the ſubject.*

There is one curious part of the Petition which muſt forcibly ſtrike every reader. The Nabob gives preciſely the ſame account of the *duties* of inferior Rulers and Zemindars that Mr. *Pitt* gave in his celebrated Speech in the Benares Charge, a few years ago.

REPRESENTATION

AND

PETITION

FROM THE

NABOB OF THE CARNATIC.

HOUSE OF COMMONS,

Lunæ, 5°, Die Martii, 1792.

A PETITION of *Albany Wallis,* and *Richard Troward,* of *Norfolk Street* in the *Strand,* Gentlemen, was presented to the House, and read; setting forth, that his Highness the Nabob of *The Carnatic* hath, by legal and authenticated instruments, appointed

D 2 the

the Petitioners his Law Agents, in Great Britain, to conduct and manage all his law concerns, as well in Parliament as otherwiſe; and that the Petitioners, as ſuch Law Agents, in the month of *July* laſt, received from his Highneſs a Repreſentation and Petition, under his ſeal, addreſſed to the Houſe, ſtating certain facts and grievances, and praying ſuch relief as to the Houſe ſhould ſeem meet, which ſaid Repreſentation and Petition the Petitioners were directed to deliver into the hands of the Right Honourable the *Speaker* of this Houſe, together with a letter from his Highneſs, requeſting that the *Speaker* would preſent the ſaid Repreſentation and Petition to the Houſe, and which the Petitioners delivered accordingly; and that the *Speaker* hath declined to preſent the ſaid Repreſentation and Petition, and hath returned

turned the ſame to the Petitioners; and therefore praying, that they may be permitted to preſent to the Houſe the ſaid Repreſentation and Petition of his Highneſs the Nabob of *The Carnatic* through the hands of ſome Member of the Houſe.

And Mr. *Speaker* having acquainted the Houſe, that his reaſons for declining to offer the ſaid Petition of his Highneſs the Nabob of *The Carnatic* to the Houſe, did not ariſe from any reference to the contents of the ſaid Petition, but from reſpect to the courſe of the proceedings that is obſerved, when Petitions are offered to the Houſe;

Ordered,

That leave be given to preſent the ſaid Petition of his Highneſs the Nabob of *The Carnatic,* as deſired by the ſaid *Albany Wallis* and *Richard Troward.*

Then

Then a repreſentation and Petition, of his Highneſs the Nabob *Wau Lau Jau Ummeer ul Hind Omdat ul Mulk Auſuph ud Dowlah Unwer ud Dien Cawn Bahauder Zuphar Jung Sepah Saular*, Sovereign and Soubahdar of the *Carnatic Payenghaut* and *Ballaghaut*, was preſented to the Houſe, and read; ſetting forth, that the Empire of the *Moguls*, in *India*, has ſubſiſted for ſeveral ages, diſpenſing, by favour of the Almighty God, the bleſſings of a regular Government to a large diviſion of the inhabitants of the earth: that one ſupreme monarch the King of the *Moguls* rules over all the kingdoms, provinces, and dominions, of the ſaid extenſive empire: that the ſeveral kingdoms, or provinces, are governed by Princes, who derive their right to authority from the King of the *Moguls* by letters patent under the

the great ſeal of the empire and a ſolemn inveſtiture on ſuch conditions as may have been mentioned and ordered in ſuch letters patent: that inferior rulers hold certain diſtricts under the ſaid Nabobs or Princes, by whoſe Saned and ſolemn inveſtiture, the authority and rights of ſuch inferior rulers are conſtituted: that thoſe inferior rulers pay immediate allegiance and obedience, with a ſtated annual tribute, to the ſaid Nabobs, for their country, beſides performing military ſervice in war, and when peace comes paying their proportion of the expences incurred, eſtimated by the uſual amount of their reſpective revenues: that, upon the dutiful behaviour of ſuch inferior rulers, the poſſeſſions of the father are granted to the ſon, or neareſt legitimate kinſman, by a regular Saned or commiſſion, and a new inveſti-

ture,

ture, upon paying the accuſtomed fine of ſucceſſion: that no ſucceſſion is legal, nor can the ſucceſſor execute any legal act of power, until he has received ſuch Saned or commiſſion, and ſuch inveſtiture, from his immediate ſuperior the Nabob, who is Lord Paramount of the country: that, when ſuch inferior rulers or vaſſals commit any great public crime, refuſe to pay their annual tribute, evade or diſobey orders in attending their ſuperior in war with all their forces, when they abet enemies, encourage conſpiracies, or in any dangerous degree prove faithleſs to their immediate Lord, they are fined, impriſoned, or ſubjected to abſolute forfeiture, in proportion to their crimes: that, upon the extinction of the legitimate male line of ſuch vaſſals, and their lawful male kindred, their territories fall of courſe to the diſ-

poſal

poſal of their liege Lord: that the preſent Nabob of *The Carnatic*, as well as his father *Anwar ul dien Cawn Bahauder*, have been Nabobs or Princes of that kingdom or country by all the legal and regular grants and inveſtitures of the empire of the *Moguls*: that the preſent Nabob ſucceeded his father in the year of the Chriſtian æra 1749, by all the legal and regular grants, as Prince of the whole kingdom of *The Carnatic*, from the River *Criſtua*, to Cape *Comorin*: that ſuch grants, and ſuch inveſtitures, were renewed to him, with additional rights, immunities, franchiſes, and privileges, by the ſucceſſive kings of the *Moguls*, till at length, more than four and twenty years ago, he received an altumgah, or free grant, for ever, from the preſent King *Shah Allum*: that, by this grant of total independence, the allegiance of all the inhabitants of *The Carnatic*, whether natives or Europeans, was transferred to him, as it had been poſſeſſed by their former Sovereigns the Kings of *Delhi*: that the Nabob's right to the government, royalty, and dominion, of the whole *Carnatic*, has to the preſent day remained unimpaired, undiminiſhed, and unimpeached, by any act, deed, compact, treaty, conqueſt, or other ground or pretence whatſoever: that he is of right, and *de facto*, independent of any claim of ſovereignty by any Prince, Power, or State upon earth: that he is the legal, undiſputed, and acknowledged ſucceſſor of the King of the *Moguls*, in all his prerogatives and abſolute rights, over the whole *Carnatic*: that his Highneſs's father, as well as himſelf, became known to the great and gracious Kings of *Great Britain*, King *George* the

the Second, and his present Majesty King *George* the Third: that his Majesty King *George* the Second, in letters under his royal signature, and countersigned by the principal Secretary of his kingdom, promised his support to the present Nabob, as an ally who merited and should receive his protection: that, in consequence of the reciprocal friendship between the King of *Great Britain* and the Nabob, and in consideration of the undoubted rights of the latter, he was guaranteed in the possession of the whole *Carnatic*, by his *Britannic* Majesty and the *French* King, by the eleventh article of the definitive treaty of peace, concluded at Paris in the year of the Christian æra 1763: that his Majesty the King of *Great Britain*, acknowledging and considering the Nabob as Sovereign of the *Carnatic*, wrote him many gracious letters under his own royal hand, treating him as an independent Prince, and promiſing him and his family his royal and auguſt protection: that his Majeſty ſent to the Nabob, as an independent Sovereign, two ſeveral embaſſies under the Great Seal of *Great Britain*: that his rights to an abſolute independence are ſo ſelf-evident and undeniable, that the *Eaſt India* Company, when on the worſt terms with the Nabob, declared ſolemnly on their records, that they muſt acknowledge him to be a *Sovereign Prince*: that the *Engliſh Eaſt India* Company ſettled factories in the *Carnatic*, as merchants carrying on their buſineſs as ſuch under the protection of the Nabobs of the country: that, conformable to their confined ſituation, they addreſſed their immediate ſuperior the Nabob by

arzee

arzee or *petition:* that *Anwar un dien Cawn Bahauder*, the father of the present Nabob, when he arrived in his government of the *Carnatic*, found them in their factory, surrounded by something more like a garden wall than a fort: that the injustice of the French induced *Anwar ul dien Cawn Bahauder* to support the English, as well as himself, against such injustice: that *Amwar ul dien* being killed in battle by the *French*, and his son, the present Nabob, having succeeded him, *Ahmed Shah*, the King of the *Moguls*, ordered his subjects, the *English* factories settled in the *Carnatic*, to obey him the Nabob, as the mediate power between them and their sovereign, the King of the *Moguls:* that the governors of the said factories wrote arzees or petitions of thanks to the Mogul, for appointing the present

present Nabob to rule over them: that during the long war, which the ambition and injustice of the *French* raised against the Nabob, the *English* Company uniting themselves with him as faithful subjects of the Mogul, their joint exertions, which were powerfully assisted by the King of *Great Britain*, became at length victorious over all their enemies: that the Company's servants, after this signal success, solemnly, under the hand of their Governor, assured the Nabob, that their wish and resolution were to carry on their business under his protection, as they had done under the protection of former Soubadars: that the Company were so thoroughly satisfied that the Nabob was the legal and rightful Sovereign of the *Carnatic*, that they wrote circular letters to all the inferior rulers, who governed different

districts

diſtricts of the country, and who, taking advantage of the misfortunes of the late times, had acted a falſe and undutiful part towards their liege Lord: that among other rulers of leſs note, they wrote to the Rajah of *Tanjore* to obey orders and commands, ſignifying by ſuch communication, that, ſhould that vaſſal prove refractory, they, as good ſubjects, would unite their arms with thoſe of the Nabob againſt the Rajah as a rebel: that, when the buſineſs of the country was ſettled, the preſidency of *Fort Saint George*, as repreſentatives of the *Engliſh* Company, entered into an agreement with the Nabob, with this expreſſion, "being obedient to him:" that they declared that, "by the bleſſ-
"ing of God, the whole *Carnatic* was
"intirely and firmly eſtabliſhed in the
"Nabob and his poſterity:" that they ſolemnly

ſolemnly engaged, that as long as the *Engliſh* ſettlements ſhall remain in the *Deckan*, *Bengal*, and *Hindoſtan*, the Company's people are diligently to uſe their endeavours in promoting and aſſiſting the affairs of the *Carnatic*, in its obedience to the Nabob, and in maintaining firm friendſhip and regard: that the mind of the Nabob, being ſwayed by reciprocal ſentiments of regard towards the *Engliſh* Company, granted them a large jaghire, which they ſtill hold under him as Lord Paramount: that the grant of ſuch jaghire not only promoted their opulence, but raiſed them to their political ſituation in the *Carnatic*, which is that of perpetual Jaghiredars: that, after the fortunate ſettlement of the public troubles, peace, the wiſh of all good men, became the commencement of misfortune to the

Nabob:

Nabob: that the Company's ſervants having, by the powerful aid of the King of *Great Britain*, been of very ſignal and very effectual ſervice in expelling the enemies of the *Carnatic*, began to mix their hands with its internal politics: that, under the pretence of being unable to obtain juſtice by force from the Rajah of *Tanjore*, for his rebellious, treacherous, and dangerous behaviour during the war, they entered into a treaty with him: that the Nabob, deeming the terms of the treaty very far from being adequate, was very unwilling to ſign it; and that the preſident of *Fort Saint George* put the Nabob's chop by force to the ſaid treaty: that the Nabob will not aſcribe the treaty to the intereſts of individuals, but will only obſerve, that it was a glaring encroachment on his juſt and independent rights, as Sovereign of all the inhabitants of *The Carnatic:* that the Company's ſervants having forgot the object of their inſtitution, which was trade, in the length of the war turned their thoughts to other views: that, by preſſing the Nabob to pay his debt to the Company, which he had incurred for their aid, during the troubles, and that in inſtalments too large for his revenue, he was forced to involve himſelf by borrowing money of individuals at a great intereſt: that thus he became to be preſſed by nearly the ſame perſons in a double capacity; on the one ſide as managers of the public funds, on the other as partly the proprietors of the private debts: that diſtreſs thus began, and was followed up by various misfortunes: that the Company's government, on the ſcore of his diſtreſſes, aſſumed a

high

high tone, and as creditors of the Nabob began to leſſen his authority, by interfering with his government: that, to render him more ſubſervient to their own domineering ſpirit, they very induſtriouſly and ſucceſsfully concealed from the Nabob his being guaranteed in all his rights by the eleventh article of the treaty of *Paris*: that he only heard of that treaty at laſt through the humanity of an *Engliſh* gentleman, after the Preſidency of *Fort Saint George* threatened to reduce him the Nabob to a mere nominal Nabob like *him* of *Bengal*: that the Company's ſervants, availing themſelves of the Nabob's ignorance of the treaty, and of his want of acceſs to the juſtice of the *Britiſh* government and nation, preſſed and oppreſſed him as avarice or other paſſions prevailed; that they entered into a war without his consent, but in his name, and charged him with the expences of it as his war: that he was thus exposed to a double misfortune, his country being ravaged by the enemy, and being forced to extort from his exhausted subjects such sums as the servants of the Company chose to charge him with on account of their masters: that the Nabob, worn out by oppressions, and harassed by extortions, resolved to convey his complaints to the ears of his protector and the guarantee of his dominions, his Majesty the King of *Great Britain*: that he wrote a letter to the Earl of *Chatham*, then his Majesty's Minister, and who had corresponded with him the Nabob, as an ally of *Great Britain*, ten years before: that, in consequence of his letter, his Majesty was pleased to appoint an ambassador,

dor, under the Great Seal, to inquire into the grievances of the Nabob on the ſpot: that the inferior and ſubordinate rulers of provinces and diſtricts of *The Carnatic*, perceiving that the Nabob's authority was invaded by the Company's ſervants, became refractory, diſobedient, and treacherous, evading their annual tribute, refuſing their military ſervices, correſponding with rebels, and abetting enemies: that the moſt rich, and conſequently the moſt powerful, the Rajah of *Tanjore*, though highly favoured in an agreement made in the year 1762, became, perhaps, upon that very account, the leaſt attentive to his duty, and the moſt obſtinate in his public and conſtitutional delinquency: that, ſmall as the tribute was which he agreed to pay by that treaty, he evaded the payment of it by various and falſe pretences: that he he encouraged and correſponded with the rebel *Jſoph Cawn*: that he abetted the invaſion of *Hyder Ali*, and gave him money and proviſions for his army: that he invited *the Mahrattas* to *the Carnatic*, and carried on intrigues with the different *European* factories and ſettlements on the Coaſt: that he refuſed to perform his military ſervices when war was in the country, though bound to give it upon the requiſition of the ſuperior: that as a proof of his connivance with *Hyder Alli*, that chief, when ſuperior in the field, inſiſted upon his being included as his friend in the treaty which he forced upon the ſervants of the Company at the gates of *Madras*: that he refuſed to pay his proportion of the expences of the war, though poſſeſſed of a very ample revenue, and his country being ſituated in the very heart of *the Carnatic*,

he

he was protected from all danger by the exertions of the Nabob and the *English* nation: that the conduct of this Rajah was altogether inexcusable, will appear from the following facts: that the part of *the Carnatic* which is called *Tanjore* is, as has been just mentioned, surrounded on three sides by the rest of *the Carnatic:* that the fertility of the country depends on the river *Cavery*, which, contrary to its natural course, is forced into the province of *Tanjore*, by a mound of earth, in a place beyond its limits: that from that circumstance, and others unnecessary to be named, *Tanjore* has been always dependent on its neighbours: that when a *Hindoo* sovereign reigned over *the Carnatic*, the Naigs of *Tanjore* were his feudatories, vassals, and subjects: that when the *Hindoo* empire declined, it became a

part

part of the conqueſt of the *Patan* kingdoms of *the Decan*; and that when trouble and invaſions directed their forces and attention to another quarter, *Tanjore*, never intended, by its ſituation and nature, to be a ſeparate government, became dependent on the Rajahs of *Tritchinopoly*: that in the years of the Christian æra 1686 and 1687, that great, wiſe, and fortunate king of the *Moguls*, the illuſtrious *Allumgeer*, having reduced the kingdoms of *The Decan*, became ſovereign of *The Carnatic*: that *Allumgeer*, having conſtituted one of his nobles *Zulphuear Cawn Behauder* Nabob of *Arcot* and *The Carnatic*, ordered him to reduce the Naig of *Tanjore*, who had raiſed troubles by abetting the deſigns of the enemies of the king: that when the ſaid Nabob was on his march to diſplace the Naig, the ſaid Naig made the moſt

most humble submissions to him the Nabob as his immediate superior: that, in consequence of his submission, he was restored to his government, upon the usual terms given to feudatories and vassals; that is, upon paying an annual tribute of £. 300,000. besides performing military service, with all his forces: that to the said Naig, whose name was *Sahu-je*, succeeded *Shurfa-je*; and to him *Babu-Saheb*, both of whom paid their annual tribute, performed their military services, besides paying the usual fine of succession upon their respective investitures to their immediate liege Lord, the Nabob of *Arcot*: that, after some troubles, which were settled and composed by the decision of the Divan, or Council of the Nabob of *The Carnatic*, *Sahu-je*, the second of the name, became Rajah, by the commission,

 creation,

creation, and inveſtiture of the ſaid Nabob: that *Sahu-je*, becoming diſobedient and refractory, was afterwards imprisoned by his liege Lord *Sepadar Ali*, Nabob of *Arcot*, who made his own preceptor, *Sheik Aſſud*, Governor of *Tanjore*: that, in troubles which followed, *Sahu-je* was again reſtored; but, being a ſecond time deprived of *Tanjore*, one *Pertaub Sing* was raiſed to the dignity of Rajah, by Saned of *Abdalla Cawn*, Nabob of *The Carnatic*; in which he was afterwards confirmed by the Nabob *Anwar ul Dien Cawn*, the father of the preſent Nabob: that *Pertaub Sing* becoming negligent in paying his tribute, and otherwiſe refractory, *Anwar ul Dien Cawn* Nabob of *The Carnatic*, was obliged to march againſt him, and, having defeated and chaſtiſed him, received him to his protection, upon

upon paying his arrears, and the expence of the expedition: that the *English* Company's Government fired their guns, and made other demonſtrations of joy, when they heard of the Nabob's victory over his vaſſal, and congratulated him in an addreſs on that victory: that when the Nabob was unfortunately killed in battle by the *French*, and other rebels, in *July* 1749, much trouble enſued in *The Carnatic*: that a war being kindled, in which the *French* aſſiſted a falſe Nabob, and the *Engliſh*, as good ſubjects of the Empire, having ſtood forth in ſupport of the legal Nabob, his preſent Highneſs of *The Carnatic*, *Pertaub Sing*, proved falſe to his immediate Lord: that he evaded the payment of his annual tribute, and refuſed compliance upon requiſition of the military ſervices, he was bound to perform by

 the

the nature of his tenure: that he ſecretly abetted the *French*, and correſponded with their rulers, whilſt he amuſed, betrayed, and deceived, his Lord Paramount, and his friends the *Engliſh*: that by theſe means he ſaved his revenue, and became rich, and thus, by his influence or his power, induced the *Engliſh* Preſidency to make the ſaid treaty of 1762: that, however, the treaty of 1762 related only to matters of account, and the future amount of the annual peiſhcuſh, or tribute; and that, conſequently, it left the conſtitutional rights of the Nabob over *Tanjore* unimpaired and entire: that *Pertaub Sing* dying in *December* 1763, his ſon *Tulja-je*, in conſequence of the Nabob's promiſe to the father, was raiſed by ſaned and inveſtiture to the *Putt* of *Tanjore*, upon paying the uſual fine of

ſucceſſion

ſucceſſion to his Lord: that the firſt act of his power was to aſſaſſinate all his legitimate male relations, making himſelf the laſt of his family: that he was as perfidious, and more abandoned than his father, was guilty of every public breach of duty, allegiance, and faith: that the Directors of the *Eaſt India* Company were ſo much offended at his conduct, that they ſent poſitive orders to their ſervants at *Madras* to aſſiſt the Nabob in bringing the ſaid *Tulja-je*, his vaſſal, to a ſevere account, for his multiplied delinquencies: that thoſe orders were not executed by the preſidency of *Fort Saint George*, on account of the political ſtate of the ſurrounding powers when the orders arrived, the Nabob himſelf being unwilling to drive matters to any extremity on the ſame account: that the Rajah, continuing a ſyſtem of delinquency,

delinquency, presumed to take up arms against his neighbours and fellow vassals, the subjects and dependents of the Nabob: that the *English* Presidency, as well as the Nabob, when they remonstrated against the conduct of *Tulja-je*, were treated by him with inattention, insolence, and contempt: that the Nabob and the Presidency, were obliged, through necessity, to have recourse to arms: that their troops, in conjunction with the eldest son of the Nabob, attacked and besieged *Tanjore*, and, a breach being made, the Rajah agreed to terms equally dissatisfactory to the Nabob and to the Presidency: that the besiegers had scarce removed their troops from the sight of the Rajah, when he began, or rather renewed, his connection with *Hyder* and the *Mahrattas*, then the enemies of the *Carnatic*: that he continued

tinued his intrigues with the *French*, *Dutch*, and *Danes*: that he not only left unperformed the articles of his late agreement, but broke the treaty of 1762, by evading the payment of his tribute, the ſettlement of accounts, and the amount of the annual tribute, being the ſole objects of that treaty: that, while he refuſed to pay his juſt peiſhcuſh to his ſuperior, he aided the enemies of that ſuperior with money, proviſions, and every ſpecies of aſſiſtance, to induce and enable them to invade the *Carnatic*: that the Preſidency of *Fort Saint George*, urged by the neceſſity of preventing the dangerous efforts of the Rajah in the very heart of the *Carnatic*, again joined their forces with thoſe of the Nabob, to chaſtiſe, and, ſhould he prove obſtinate, to reduce entirely this refractory and hoſtile vaſſal: that knowing

ing the tenure of the Company in the country, and that they had no right to interfere but as guardians of the public ſafety, they ſolemnly declared that they only acted as auxiliaries in the expedition: that they ſtipulated the conqueſt, if any conqueſt ſhould be made, ſhould belong to, and be put in poſſeſſion of, the Nabob, the principal in the war: that accordingly the expence of the expedition ſhould be paid by him, as he only was to derive any benefit from the ſucceſs which might follow: that the capital and the country ſhould remain in his hands, in the double capacity of conqueror and Lord Paramount, for that as the Company did not appear as principals in the war, they had no claim to the rewards of victory: that under ſuch ſtipulations, and many others of a ſimilar kind, too tedious to mention,

tion, the united forces of the Nabob and the Company, took *Tanjore*, the capital of the province of that name: that the Rajah, having alienated a part of the country to the *Dutch*, without the knowledge or consent of his liege Lord, the Presidency declared that their duty would not be fully performed, without placing the country, as well as the capital, in the hands of the Nabob: that the Nabob, to prevent the effusion of blood, and every pretence of a difference between the *English* and *Dutch*, agreed to pay to the latter the money which they had advanced to the Rajah, or pretended to have advanced, for the districts in their possession: that thus the province of *Tanjore*, independent of his rights as superior, became the undoubted property of the Nabob, as the acknowledged and undeniable principal in a war, which terminated in conqueſt, the moſt indiſputable and irreverſible title that can be acquired by the law of nature and nations: that *Tanjore*, thus acquired, remained and flouriſhed in the hands of the Nabob for more than two years: that the Company, ſwayed by motives different from any adherence to juſtice, or public faith, interfered with the moſt ſacred rights of their ſuperior in *The Carnatic*, and reſtored as principals a conqueſt, in the making of which they were paid as mercenaries: that, with innumerable aggravations of injuſtice, they took to themſelves the very diſtricts which the Nabob had redeemed, with a large ſum, from the *Dutch*, and that ſo regardleſs were they of the ſmalleſt conſtitutional rights of the Lord Paramount, that they took no care for the diſcharging of the ſmall tribute ſti-

pulated

pulated by the treaty of 1762: that the flagrant breach of the public faith, made by the reſtoration of *Tanjore*, was followed by various and grievous encroachments on the remaining rights of the Nabob: that he was ſtript of all dignity and authority among his ſubjects, by being denied the freedom of entertaining a few troops for enforcing the laws, and protecting his perſon: that, contrary to the privilege of a Prince and Sovereign, his family and ſervants have been wantonly inſulted by the operation of the Company's law court within his territories, and even within his reſidence: that, contrary to the laws of nations, *The Carnatic* has been involved in war, without either the conſent or participation of its Sovereign; and that he was obliged to pay a very large portion of the expence: that although the province of

Tanjore yields a great revenue, and ought to yield more, no proportion of he expences of the war was demanded of the Rajah: that, when peace was concluded in *The Carnatic*, the name of the Nabob, the Sovereign of the country, was not mentioned in the treaty: while, to add to this severe indignity, the names of some of his vassals and dependents were inserted, and their interests included in that treaty: that although the war was not the Nabob's war, to manifest his attachment to the *English* interests, he agreed to assign his revenue towards maintaining it into the hands of the Company's servants, upon certain stipulations and conditions, and for a time limited: that as soon as the collection of the revenue came into the hands of the Company's servants, they seized the whole authority of the Nabob, who was thereby

thereby diſgraced in the eyes of his ſubjects, and all the powers of India: that, although the Nabob was ſeverely aggrieved by ſuch invaſion and oppreſſion, the Company were not benefited by the meaſure, the country yielding much leſs under the new collectors, than it had done to the Nabob: that the Nabob, and his family, and dependants, were reduced to want and diſtreſs by the ſmallneſs and irregularity of the payment of the portion allotted for his ſubſiſtence; and that he languiſhed for ſeveral years under the indignity and preſſure of his misfortunes: that, when peace was eſtabliſhed between the crowns of *Great Britain* and *France*, his Sacred Majeſty the King of *Great Britain* agreed to intercede with his ally the Nabob for the ceſſion of additional territories to the *French* on the Coaſt: that, notwithstanding this implied intercession, considerable districts of the *Carnatic* were delivered to the French by the Presidency of *Fort Saint George*, without asking either the consent or acquiescence of the Nabob: that orders were sent from *England* in 1784, which arrived in *June* 1785, to restore his country and revenue to the Nabob: that in these orders it was mentioned, that the Nabob should consent to pay annually twelve lacks of pagodas to his public and private creditors: that the government of *Fort Saint George* demanded four lacks of pagodas more for the current expences, in all sixteen lacks of pagodas: that the Nabob complained of the burden of this sum, as too great for the ability of his country, fresh from the devastations of war: that he signified his wishes, as the public expence of defence muſt of neceſſity be defrayed, to have his annual payments of debts leſſened, from which little inconvenience would ariſe, as it would be only extending the payment of a debt, for which intereſt would be regularly given, to a ſmall portion of time, beyond what was originally intended: that this would give eaſe to the diſtreſſed ſubjects of the *Carnatic*, and enable the Sovereign to reſtore the country to its former proſperity, by encouraging the cultivation: that orders, which muſt be allowed to be founded on the principles of equity, were ſent to the Preſidency of *Fort Saint George*, that the Company, in the proportion to the revenue on the Coaſt, ſhould pay their ſhare of the public expence: that, on this principle, the Nabob's proportion, under a wrong eſtimate of his revenue, was calculated at nine

lacks

lacks of pagodas: that this ſum, added to the twelve lacks paid to his public and private creditors, increaſed his annual kiſts to twenty-one lacks of pagodas: that his nett receipts, even in the very beſt years, and in the moſt proſperous times, ſeldom amounted to that ſum: that they had fallen much below that amount, through the devaſtations of war, and a general and deſtructive drought: that the kiſts, ſtipulated to be paid to the Company, are far from being the whole of the expences of the Nabob: that to keep his country from abſolute ruin, he muſt maintain public works, repair tanks and water courſes, and give money to the poor ryots, to enable them to cultivate their lands: that he is bound, by every tye, to pay ſums, for charitable uſes, to ſupport his relations and their families, together

with

with the old ſervants and dependents of himſelf and his father: that, beſides, he is obliged to ſupport ſome kind of decent kind of dignity, as Prince of the country, and to maintain a numerous family of children: that the fundamental laws, on which the rights of the Nabob of *the Carnatic* are founded, are deeply affected with reſpect to *the jagbire* and diſtrict of *Arni*: that *Zulphucar Cawn Bahauder*, Nabob of the *Carnatic*, confirmed one *Conary Row* in that jaghire on the uſual conditions: that the ſaid *Conary Row* was to take care of, and to keep the fort in repair, to pay monthly the garriſon, to ſend their receipts to the King's office as vouchers, to treat the ſoldiers with kindneſs, and to pay every attention to their rights, to engage their fidelity and attachment to the King: that the ſaid

Conary Row ſhould pay a yearly peiſh-cuſh into the King's Treaſury : and, in the event of a war in the *Carnatic*, to pay his ſhare of the expences thereof, in proportion to the revenue of the jaghire, as ſettled by the Nabob of the King: " that, in caſe he ſhould act con-" trary to thoſe duties, he muſt look " upon himſelf as diſpoſſeſſed, and under " the diſpleaſure of the King :" that during the troubles, which infeſted the *Carnatic* for ſeveral years, the Killedar of *Arni* took advantage of the misfortunes of the times, by withdrawing his obedience : that he oppreſſed the people of the jaghire, being under no apprehenſion of controul : that he attacked his neighbours and fellow ſubjects, and gave protection to robbers, murderers, and all criminals who fled from juſtice : that he was guilty of all the crimes that

conſtitute

conſtitute public delinquency, in the eyes of any regular government: that the preſidency of *Fort Saint George* concurred in opinion with the Nabob, as to the expediency of removing the Killedar: that he was accordingly deprived of his command, and the military ſtipend, ariſing from the jaghire, was taken away, but that he and his family were provided with an allowance, for an honourable ſubſiſtence: that, notwithſtanding the concurrence of the Preſidency in depriving ſo dangerous a man of power, they reſtored to him the emoluments formerly allotted for the military ſervice of the ſtate: that the fort and its expence were left to the Nabob, and the whole revenue given to the Killedar and his friends: that an ample revenue, received without deduction, promoted diſputes and diſſentions among themſelves: that the circles of trouble ſpreading to the neighbouring country, the ſervants of the Company, as well as the Nabob, were alarmed: that the Preſidency accordingly gave their advice and concurrence to the Nabob in reſuming the jaghire: that the Nabob accordingly reſumed it, and paid a monthly allowance to the Killedar and his family, till *Hyder Ali*, having ravaged *Arni*, with other parts of the *Carnatic*, in the year 1780, deprived it of all reſources: that *Arni*, with the reſt of the *Carnatic*, fell under the management of the ſervants of the Company by the deed of aſſignment: that when the reſt of the *Carnatic* was reſtored to the Nabob, *Arni* was not reſtored: that ſuch conduct is an unjuſtifiable interference with the independent rights of the Nabob: that, beſides his

loſs

loſs of revenue, he is diſhonoured, by the meaſure, in the eyes of India; as the nature of things, as well as the matter of fact, proves, that the Killedar could not poſſibly have been permitted to have any indefeaſible right, in a place within a few miles of the capital of *The Carnatic*: that on the 31ſt of *January* 1787, *Tulga-ge*, Rajah of *Tanjore*, died, leaving none exiſting of the legitimate line of his family: that the Nabob, as Lord Paramount of the country, made a requiſition to the Company's governments in *India*, to place *Tanjore* under his adminiſtration, according to the univerſal laws of the eaſt: that the view of the Nabobs's requiſition was, not only the preſervation of the undoubted and indiſputable rights of his government and ſovereignty, but to ſecure the peace of *The Carnatic*, which nature intended, and

and policy required, ſhould be under one government: that, adding advantage to juſtice, the Nabob made propoſals, which could not fail to render the affairs of the *Engliſh* nation, on the coaſt, proſperous: that the whole revenue of *Tanjore* is eſtimated, at preſent, at no more than ten lacks of pagodas; which may juſtly be aſcribed to the looſe, profligate, and oppreſſive government of the country, after it was unjuſtly wreſted from the hands of the Nabob, in 1776: that the Company only receive, out of that ſum, four lacks of pagodas, for the general defence: that the Nabob propoſed, that the *whole revenue* of *Tanjore* (after defraying the charges of collection, and providing ſuch a reaſonable ſubſiſtence for the remains of *Tulja-je*'s family, as the Company's government ſhould think proper),

proper) ſhould be appropriated, and ſet apart, for the military ſervice of *The Carnatic*: that to render this offer more determinate and explicit, the Nabob engaged to realize, the firſt year eleven lacks; the ſecond year thirteen lacks; and from the third year fifteen lacks of pagodas annually, to be paid to the Company, and to be applied to the general expence: that this laſt mentioned ſum is one third more than the whole eſtimated revenue of the country at preſent; and near four times as much as the Company now receive from *Tanjore*, towards the public defence: that the Company's governments acceding to the Nabob's propoſals would perfectly ſecure *The Carnatic* from all foreign invaſion: that the public finances would flouriſh, and the army be formidable: that the Company, inſtead of being almoſt deſ-

titute

titute of commerce, as at present, might apply their whole revenue, amounting to near twenty lacks of pagodas, to the purposes of investment: that a subject of such importance will prove an excuse for repetitions, that the Nabob is the Sovereign and Lord Paramount of *Tanjore*, which was left without heirs, by the death of *Tulja-je:* that, by the laws of *India*, and those of all countries in the world where the feudal government exists, a territory left without heirs reverts to the sovereign: that the *East India* Company are no more than subjects in *Hindostan:* that in *Bengal* they are Dewans; but only Jaghirdars in *The Carnatic:* that neither as Dewans of *Bengal*, which country hath nothing to do with *The Carnatic*; nor as Jaghirdars on the coast, where their very tenure marks them as subjects, they have the smallest shadow

ſhadow of a title to interfere with the conſtitutional rights of their Lord Paramount: that, however, the conſtitutional rights of the Nabob, with reſpect to *Tanjore*, were overlooked or neglected: that the offers of an immenſe advantage to the Company and *Britiſh* nation were diſregarded: that a natural ſon of the late *Pertaub Sing*, who had been more than twelve years a priſoner, was placed in the government of *Tanjore*: that neither a ſaned of ſucceſſion, nor an inveſtiture were either aſked from, nor given by, the Nabob; without which no legal government can poſſibly exiſt in *Tanjore*: that, thus the Nabob is grievouſly injured, in his neareſt, deareſt, and moſt ſacred rights: that the Company and *Britiſh* nation are much injured in point of finance: that an example of encroachment is exhibited to the eyes of all *India*; and a government eſtabliſhed, in one of its provinces, which, having its foundation on no right, cannot diſpenſe juſtice, the great end of all government: that, when the treaty of *February* 1787, was negotiating between the Nabob and the *Madras* government, he repreſented to them, that the ſums demanded from him were of ſuch a vaſt magnitude as he was fully convinced his country was by no means able to bear; and Governor *Campbell*, in conſequence of the Nabob's repreſentations, agreed, in a public letter, previous to the execution of the treaty, that an abatement of two lacks of pagodas *per annum* ſhould be made in his kiſts, if the revenues were formed unequal to the payment: that the Company's ſervants have refuſed to allow him this annual abatement, though the Nabob offered to ſub-

mit

mit the accounts of his receipts to the inſpection of ſuch perſons as the Governor and Council ſhould think proper to appoint for that purpoſe: that by the ſaid treaty of 1787, it was ſtipulated, that in the event of any failure in the kiſts from the want of rain, or other unforeſeen calamities, a deduction ſhould be made to the extent of the injury which the revenues might thereby ſuſtain: that the Company's ſervants have alſo refuſed to conform to this ſtipulation, and to allow him any deduction in his kiſts on account of failure in his revenues from the want of rain, though it was well known to them that they had ſuffered in a very great degree from an unuſual drought of four ſucceſſive years, and their own jaghire had ſuffered greatly from the ſame cauſe, and for which they had granted remiſſion to

K 2 their

their own rentors: that by the ſame treaty it was agreed and ſtipulated, that the Nabob ſhould be furniſhed annually with an accurate account, ſhewing the number of troops maintained, and the names and ſituations of the garriſons ſupported by the annual contributions, and particularly the troops and garriſons maintained by the nine lacks of pagodas annually contributed by his Highneſs to the general defence: that it is now upwards of three and a half years ſince the execution of that treaty, yet the Nabob has not been furniſhed with any account whatever, not even of the dividends made to his private creditors; and though he is to pay nearly one half of the expences of the late war in *The Carnatic*, and the Company receive yearly about four lacks of pagodas under that head, yet they will not aſcertain the *quantum*

of

of thoſe expences, or furniſh him with any account to ſhew when his payments therein are to have an end: that, by the 15th article of the aforeſaid treaty, it is alſo ſtipulated, that, whenever the Company ſhall enter into any negotiations, wherein the intereſts of *The Carnatic* and its dependencies, may be concerned, the Preſident in Council of *Fort Saint George* ſhall communicate the proceedings to his Highneſs the Nabob of *The Carnatic*, as the firm ally of the Company, and that he ſhall be informed of all meaſures which ſhall relate to the declaring of war, or making peace with any of the Princes of *Hindoſtan*, ſo far as the intereſts of *The Carnatic* may be immediately concerned therein; and the name of his Highneſs ſhall be inſerted in all treaties regarding *The*

Carnatic:

Carnatic: that great preparations for war were made for ſeveral months together, and negotiations entered into with the *Nizam* and the *Mahratta* States, and treaties finally made with thoſe powers by the Company's Governments in *India:* that ſo far from conforming to that article of the treaty, the Nabob was not informed of any of the proceedings regarding thoſe negotiations, until after they had been concluded, and the treaties executed, and even then no further than being furniſhed with copies of the treaties with the *Nizam* and the *Mahrattas*, in which neither his name nor *The Carnatic* are ſo much as mentioned: that the army has been aſſembled, and hoſtilities have been commenced againſt *Tippoo*, for ſeveral months paſt, without

out giving the Nabob any information relative to the operations of the war, though he is expected to pay nearly one half the expence thereof: that the grain of his country, in which the greatest part of his revenues consists, the ploughing cattle, and the husbandmen, were seized for the use of the army, whereby he was deprived of the means of realizing the actual resources of his country: that, after having taken these steps, the Company's Government at *Madras* drew up an incorrect and unjust account against the Nabob, by suppressing the reduction to be made on the new arrangement and the allowance to be granted by treaty for failure of crops in bad seasons, whereby they made appear a large balance in favour of the Company, and, without so much as comparing

paring it with the Nabob's ſtatement, thus tranſmitted it to the Government General of *Bengal*, which was thereby erroneouſly led to order the ſequeſtration of his country: that, in direct breach of the aforeſaid treaty of 1787, and in defiance of the laws of nations, they carried the ſaid orders of the Government General into the moſt rigorous execution, ſeized the Adminiſtration of his country by force of arms, committed acts of barbarity towards many of his principal ſervants and ſubjects, men of family and diſtinction, throughout the countries, and, in the face of all the Princes and powers, and the *European* nations, in *India*, in the face of his enemies, and of his own ſubjects and dependants, have indelibly injured his honour, inſulted his dignity, and reduced him

him to the mere ſhadow of the Prince of *The Carnatic*: that the Nabob has now been the moſt faithful and ſtedfaſt ally of the *Engliſh* nation, during a period of near fifty years: that he has gone hand in hand with them at all times of adverſity as well as proſperity, and has devoted his whole life and fortune to their welfare: that, after all, inſtead of enjoying repoſe and tranquillity which he had expected would have been the reward of his long and faithful attachment to the *Engliſh* nation, his latter days are embittered with aggravated misfortune and affliction, and his grey hairs treated with deriſion and contempt: that there are many other grievances under which the Nabob labours, but which the eſtabliſhing a general line, that muſt not be tranſgreſſed, will remove: that, in ſetting forth the griev-ances he has explained, he has avoided to accuſe or blame individuals: that re-dreſs is his object, and not revenge; and that, content with receiving juſtice for the future, he wants no retribution for paſt injuries: that he is willing to aſcribe ſome public encroachments upon his rights to the Company's being ignorant of the limits of their own; and far be it from his heart to lay to the charge of a great nation, whom he eſteems, ad-mires, and loves, thoſe enormities, en-croachments, and oppreſſions, which paſſions of various kinds have ſuggeſted to individuals: that the Nabob of *The Carnatic* ſends this his Petition to the Honourable the Commons of *Great Britain* in Parliament aſſembled, as the Company of Merchants of *England*

trading

trading to *The East Indies*, and their concerns, are peculiarly under their inspection and controul; and therefore praying the House to take the premises into their consideration, and to do in them as to the House shall seem fit.

FINIS.

www.ingramcontent.com/pod-product-compliance
Lightning Source LLC
Chambersburg PA
CBHW020337090426
42735CB00009B/1570

* 9 7 8 3 3 3 7 1 5 6 7 8 7 *